The Art I

Inspiring Children to be Creative

SUE TRUSLER

First published in the United Kingdom in 2022 by
The Choir Press
ISBN 978-1-78963-341-2

Acknowledgements

Thanks to Penarth Library who ignited the spark for The Art Family to be created, by inviting me to run a childrens art event.

Thanks to Michael Heppell and members of his Write That Book Masterclass, who have supported and encouraged me.

Thanks to Choir Press for their publishing guidance and patience.

Endorsement

This book is perfect for parents of young children to start encouraging creativity in a fun and easily understandable way. All children love to draw and this book really helps them develop their artistic skills, they are going to love the Art Family characters and making magic colours.

Stefanie Lillie
Author and Grandmother

This is a terrific book for young children to learn the very basics of art and begin their creative journey. A handy section for adults is included with plenty of ideas to encourage and develop children's creativity. Definitely one for my little grandkids!

Rachael Trask
Author

This book is fun. An excellent way to get children excited about creating their own art. The vibrant colours, fun illustrations and easy to follow instructions make this a must have. Inspiring creativity is the gift of this book.

Sharon Sanders
Transformation Consultant Education and Learning

Welcome to The Art Family, designed to capture the imagination of young children, as they begin to explore their artistic creativity. The characters are fun and easy to recognise, linking to specific styles of lines and shapes. The Art Family lead the way to making patterns, learning about colours and creating pictures. There are a range of ideas for adults to build upon, encouraging children to create their own Art Family, with lots of other linked activities.

Having written a book encouraging adults to start painting, I am now keen to share my passion for art, to inspire children to have fun being creative.

Sue Trusler

The Art Family are all very special, made of different lines and shapes.

They all love painting and having fun.

I wonder who we are going to meet first.

Smooth Art is made of lines that can be straight or curved, but never broken or bumpy.

Smooth Art lines are super for round footballs and straight goal posts.

Wobbly Art is always moving and
never stays straight.

Wobbly Art lines are wonderful, for waves and pirate flags.

Dash Art is made of little lines and spaces. Their pattern can be straight or curved, but they never join up.

Dash Art lines are perfect for painting fantastic fireworks.

Spiky Art has lots of sharp points,
that stick out all over the place.

Spiky Art lines are sharp and pointed, perfect for big dinosaurs and small hedgehogs.

Curly Art never stops going round
and round, in curls and loops.

Curly Art lines are cute, for woolly sheep and posh poodles.

Dot Art is made from lots of spots that never join up.

Dot Art shapes can be large or small, ideal for rain and spotty monsters.

Now we know all the Art Family lines and shapes.

Can You draw them?

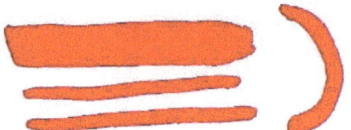

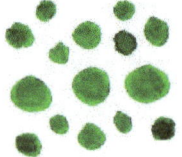

So, let's look at some special colours.

White is the lightest and can be used for ice cream and snowflakes.

Black is the darkest for spiders and bats.

There are also three magic colours.

Red   Yellow   Blue

Let's see what they can do.

Mixing magic Red and Blue

makes a new colour called Purple.

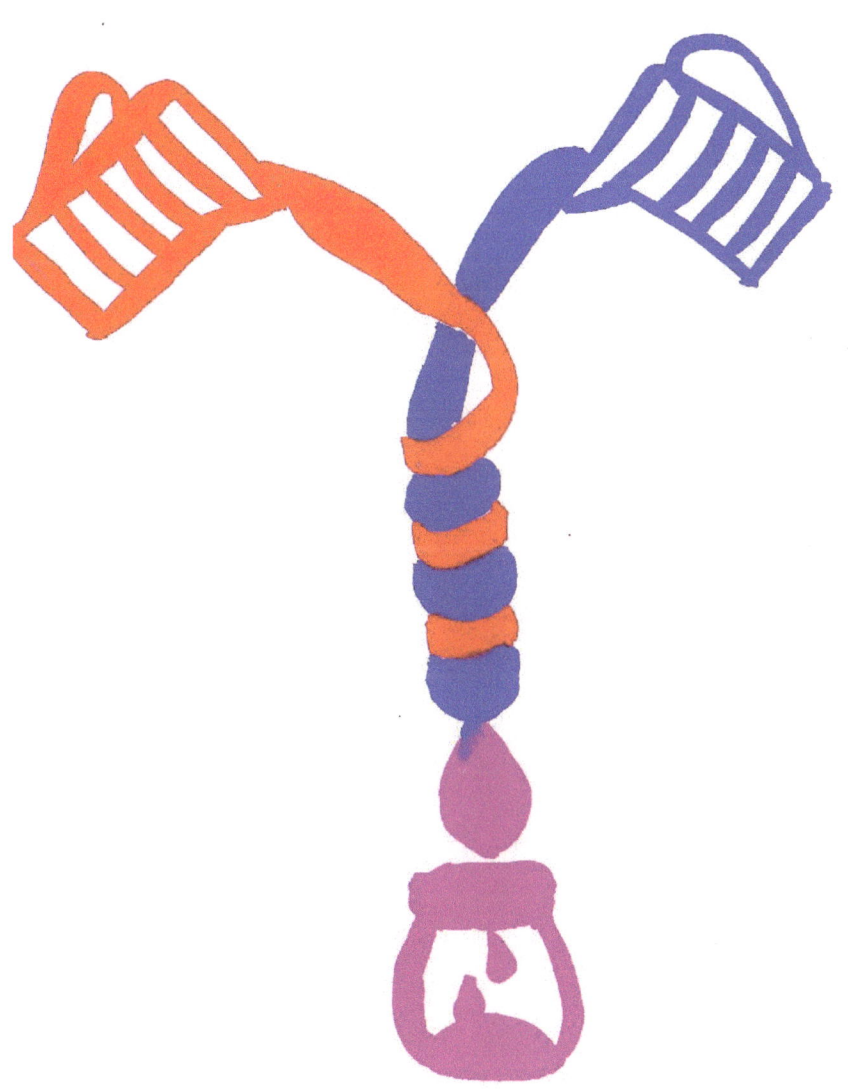

Mixing magic Red and Yellow makes a new colour called Orange

Mixing magic Yellow and Blue
makes a new colour called Green.

Now it's time to have some fun with all the Art Family lines and shapes, using all the different colours.

Can you name all the colours?

Before we begin to have fun painting, lets see if you can remember the Art Family names.

Do you know who is missing?

The Art Family would like to share some ideas for you to try.

Smooth Art loves the city, with tall straight buildings.

Smooth Art has help from Wobbly Art, to make some flags.

Green, Orange and Red are used for traffic lights.

Black and White make a stripy zebra crossing.

Let's see if you can draw some tall buildings, with Smooth Art lines.

Wobbly Art likes being at the seaside, with lots of wobbly waves.

Smooth Art helps to make boats that go up and down on the waves.

Dash Art uses lots of yellow, to help the sun to shine.

All the colours make the seaside a bright and happy place.

Let's see if you can paint a sunny
seaside picture with Wobbly Art
lines.

Dash Art likes to make lots of patterns and pictures, with dashes all over the place.

Sometimes Smooth Art draws shapes for Dash Art to fill with patterns.

Dash Art likes to use lots of colours to make the shapes look bright and cheerful.

Let's see what patterns you can
make with Dash Art lines.

Spiky Art loves high mountains with big spikes.

Sometimes Dash Art helps to make paths for walking.

Curly Art is very good at making fluffy clouds above the mountains.

Smooth Art and Curly Art work together, to make the trees that grow on the mountains.

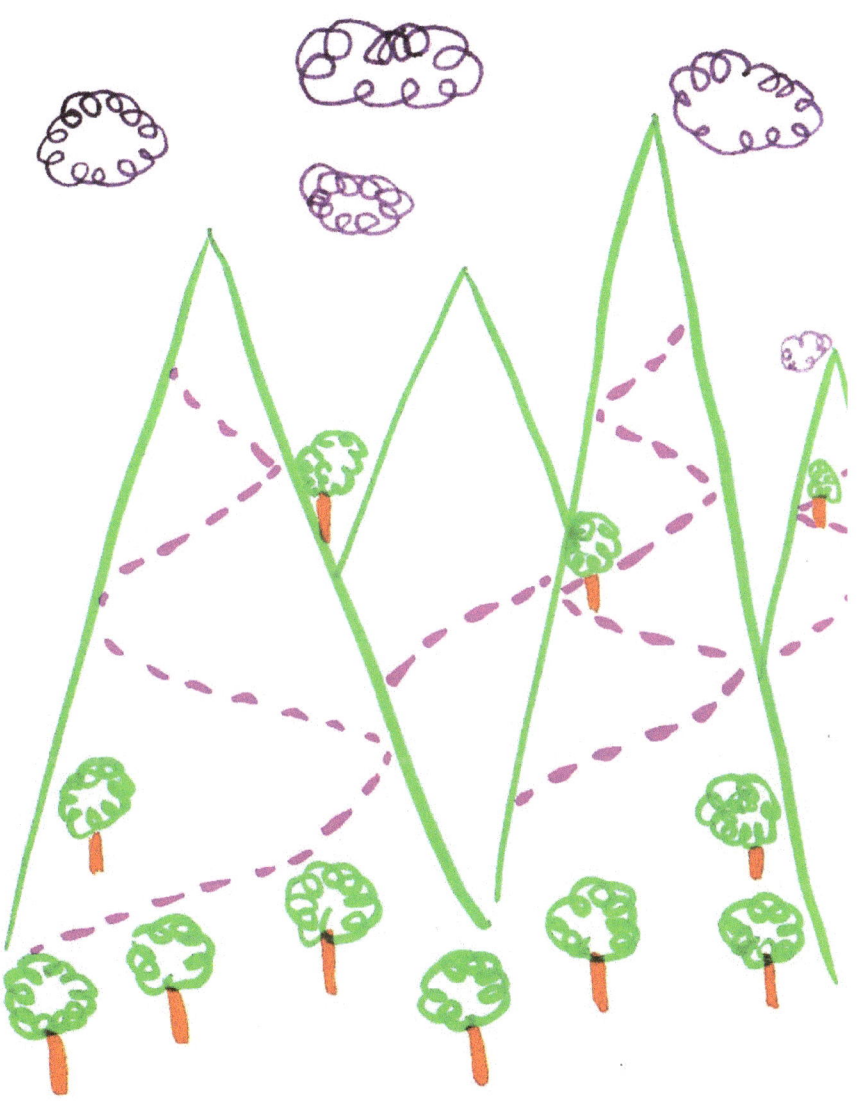

Let's see if you can paint some
mountains with **Spiky Art** lines.

Curly Art loves painting warm woolly jumpers.

Curly Art also likes painting matching bobble hats, that keep people warm in wintertime.

Using lots of colours makes the jumpers all look different.

Maybe Curly Art could try making a jumper with different colours all mixed up?

Let's see if you can paint some woolly jumpers with Curly Art lines.

Dot Art likes to have fun making everything very spotty.

Dot Art uses lots of colours all mixed up, for painting tiny dots and big spots.

Smooth Art likes to help, making beautiful butterflies in all shapes and sizes, so Dot Art can make them super smart and spotty.

Let's see if you can paint some
butterflies and make them look
pretty with Dot Art.

The Art Family have shared all their favourite lines and colours.

Now it's time for you to have fun making your own pictures.

Materials and Ideas for Adults

Whilst the mixing of colours is best using paints, there are other fun art materials for creating pictures.

Chalk, Wax Crayons, Coloured Pencils

As well as brushes for painting there are some fun alternatives,

Sponges /Sponge sticks, Fingers &Toes, Feathers & Sticks

To help very young ones, you can cut out a stencil, for them to draw the head and eyes, to start their Art Family members.

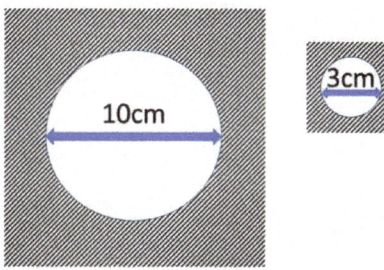

Getting little hands ready for painting, can be used to help learn the Art Family names and styles.

Smooth

Place hands flat on table, slide forwards and back, then side to side.

Wobbly

Place finger tips on table then wiggle like waves.

Dash

Hold hands above table and make quick clawing movements, scratching surface.

Spiky

Clench fists tight then quickly open out fingers and thumb.

Curly

Wave hands around making large and small circles in the air.

Dot

Tap fingertips on table like playing a piano, fast and slow. Quietly for rain drops and loud for monster spots.

To appreciate the use of colour, create an abstract page using all six Art Family styles in one colour.

Then repeat using a different colour for each of the six styles.

Once completed, compare the single colour painting with the vibrant multi coloured one.

Ask which one they like the best and why?

Being Creative with a Group of Children

Give each child a different colour and a sheet of paper. Ask them to paint just the first Art Family style then pass their paper clockwise to the next child. Now everyone paints the next Art Family style. Repeat for each Art Family member so the paper is passed on 5 times.

An alternative is for each child to keep their paper and pass on the paint pot and brush.

This adds a bit of fun as well as using far less pots of paint and brushes.

Questions can be asked to see which of the Art Family would be good for painting different things.

Rainbow - Smooth Art

Star - Spiky Art

Rain - Dot Art

The question can be turned around, by asking what would each Art Family member be good at painting.

Curly Art - Sheep

Dash Art - Grass

Wobbly Art - Waves

These types of questions, can be used with colours as well.

Remember art is about being creative so grass doesn't have to be green, particularly if it's on another planet or a distant magic land.

Once the different Art Family shapes can be recognised, there is opportunity to make up new members.

New Smooth Art

New Wobbly Art

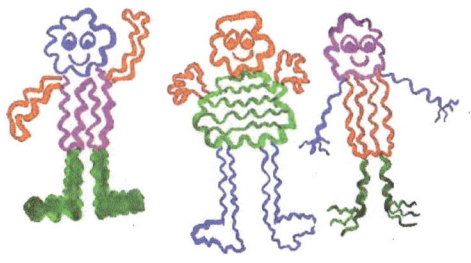

Also try combining Art Family members.

Dot Art, Wobbly Art & Spiky Art.

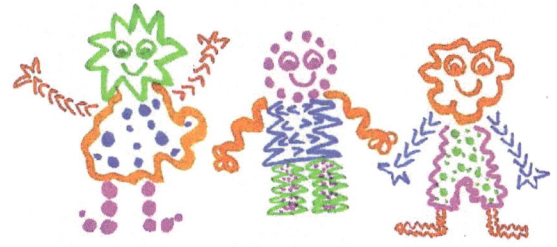

The Art Family can have their own pets, cars, houses, gardens etc.

In reverse, drawings can be made and children have to guess which animal or object, belongs to each of The Art Family.

Learning Primary and Secondary Colours.

Children can choose their 3 favourite Art Family members, to paint in the magic colours Red, Yellow and Blue.

Next, show what colour would be made if they mixed Red with Yellow, Blue with Red or Yellow with Blue.

Be Inspired, have Fun and be Creative.

CPSIA information can be obtained
at www.ICGtesting.com
Printed in the USA
LVHW070859100922
728014LV00017B/511